My Big Bug

by Larry Kelly

Illustrated by Ann Iosa

MW01046945

Target Skill Review

Scott Foresman
is an imprint of

PEARSON

My big bug is a mess.
Can Wes fix it?

"Yes," said Wes. "I can fix it.
It is fun to fix a big bug."

It is fun to fix a big bug.

It is the best.

Wes will tap it.

He taps the big bug.

Wes will rap on it.

He raps on the big bug.

Wes will mix red and yellow.
Wes will dot it on.

Look at the big bug.

I like my big red and yellow bug.